CRUISE SHIPS

BOATS & SHIPS

Jason Cooper

The Rourke Corporation, Inc.
Vero Beach, Florida 32964

PHOTO CREDITS:
Courtesy Clipper Cruise Line: pages 4, 10; courtesy Cunard and Seabourn Cruise Lines: cover, pages 17, 18; courtesy Holland America Line: pages 15, 21; courtesy Star Clippers: title page, pages 7, 12; © Lynn M. Stone: pages 8, 13

CREATIVE SERVICES:
East Coast Studios, Merritt Island, Florida

EDITORIAL SERVICES:
Susan Albury

Library of Congress Cataloging-in-Publication Data

Cooper, Jason, 1942-
    Cruise ships / by Jason Cooper.
        p. cm. — (Boats)
    Includes bibliographical references (p.   ).
    Summary: Surveys the history, uses, parts, and different kinds of cruise ships.
        ISBN 0-86593-563-7
    1. Cruise ships—Juvenile literature. 2. Ocean travel—Juvenile literature.
[1. Cruise ships. 2. Ocean liners.]
I. Title II. Series: Cooper, Jason, 1942- Boats & ships
G550.C724   1999
910' .2' 02—dc21   99–15111
                                                            CIP

Printed in the USA

TABLE OF CONTENTS

CRUISE SHIPS

Have you ever wanted to travel by ship to some faraway seaport? Or, better still, to many **ports** (PORTS) on the same trip? You're not alone.

Millions of people make voyages each year on cruise ships. Cruise ships are vessels designed to carry passengers in great comfort from port to port.

Cruise ships and ocean liners are similar, but different. An ocean liner is designed to cross the sea, going from one city to another a long way off.

Here the Yorktown Clipper *glides through Misty Fjords National Monument, Alaska.*

THE FIRST CRUISE SHIPS

The idea of ships to carry passengers only is quite new. For centuries, passengers who traveled by ship shared space with **cargo** (KAR go), or freight. And those passengers weren't aboard for a pleasant cruise. They had to travel by ship because it was the only way to cross oceans. Sea travel was dangerous in the old wooden **vessels** (VEH sulz) with their tall sails. Not until 1881 was there an all-steel passenger liner.

Sleek ships under sail offer passengers a different kind of cruise. Modern sailing ships are more seaworthy than the old wooden tall masters.

True ocean liners, or passenger liners, began to appear in the late 1800s. Their first-class, or best, rooms were very comfortable. But these ships operated largely because people could neither swim nor fly across the oceans. Ship companies were not in business to visit seaports just for the fun of it.

Passengers have left their cruise ship and taken a motor raft into this icy bay on the coast of Antarctica.

CRUISING

People who choose to travel aboard oceangoing ships today do so for pleasure. People could easily take an airplane to just about any place a ship travels. But cruising is comfortable and relaxing. People travel aboard cruise ships—and ocean liners—for the fun of it!

Cruise ships generally stop at several ports during the cruise. People leave the ship to go ashore for a day of exploring. They return to the ship later in the day. The ship sails at night. By next day, a new port is in sight.

With Nantucket Clipper *anchored nearby, cruise passengers take a break to snorkel.*

The four-masted Star Flyer *sails off the coast of Thailand.*

Science and adventure cruises take passengers on learning journeys to such places as the Amazon River and Antarctica.

A big cruise ship is a home away from home. The ship serves as many as eight meals a day! Activities include movies, computers, fitness centers, photo workshops, lectures, games, dancing, and special activities for kids. No one aboard a cruise ship should be bored.

Cruise ships can take a person almost anywhere on the oceans, from the Arctic to the Antarctic.

Part of the fun of a cruise is standing on deck and watching the scenery pass by. The Maasoam *cruises along the western coast of Canada.*

PARTS OF A CRUISE SHIP

The main part of a cruise ship is its **hull** (HUHL). The hull is the shell of the ship.

Inside the hull, below the main **deck** (DEK), are engines, spaces for storage, and some passenger rooms. Above the main deck are more decks, or floors. Passenger rooms and other rooms, such as an auditorium and restaurant, are located on one deck or another.

The **bridge** (BRIJ) is high above the main deck at the front of the ship. The bridge is the area in which the captain controls the ship's **course** (KORSS), or journey.

Passengers aboard the Queen Elizabeth II *enjoy fine meals in the Carolina Dining Room.*

OCEAN LINERS

Ocean liners became popular in the early 1900s. The most famous of the early liners was the *Titanic*.

In the 1930s, England built the famous *Queen Elizabeth* and *Queen Mary*. Both of these fast, comfortable ships were nearly 1,000 feet (300 meters) long, more than the length of three football fields.

As airplanes began to transport more people over oceans in the 1950s and 1960s, most ocean liner companies gave up. The only true ocean liner afloat now is the *Queen Elizabeth II*.

The 963-foot (290 meters) *QE II* first sailed in 1969. It carries 1,700 passengers at speeds up to almost 38 miles per hour (61 kilometers per hour).

The QE II was the only true ocean liner running at the end of the 20th century.

KINDS OF CRUISE SHIPS

Cruise ships are built in several sizes. Smaller ships can reach places that larger ones can't. Small cruise ships can sneak into rivers and bays that won't hold a monster ship. Some of the biggest cruise ships are too wide to squeeze through the Panama Canal!

Passengers who want a taste of the past can choose to cruise on a tall-masted sailing ship or a steamship.

The tall masters have engines, but they are seldom needed.

The Veendam, *docked in Seattle, is typical of a big, modern cruise ship.*

THE NEW CRUISE SHIPS

As sea cruising has become more popular, cruise ships are being built bigger. Princess Cruise Line's 2,600-passenger *Grand Princess* was the biggest of cruise ships when she first sailed in May, 1998. Her "biggest" title didn't last long.

By November, 1999, Royal Caribbean International's *Voyager of the Seas* was the largest cruise ship. It holds 3,100 passengers.

Even larger ships will be launched in the 21st century. And a new ocean liner will join the *Queen Elizabeth II* on the open seas.

GLOSSARY

bridge (BRIJ) — a raised platform from which a ship can be operated and watched

cargo (KAR go) — those goods that a ship brings abroad; freight

course (KORSS) — a ship's route as it travels

deck (DEK) — the covered area across the top of a ship or boat hull; any one of the platforms, or floors, built above the bottom of a hull

hull (HUHL) — the floating shell of a boat or ship

port (PORT) — a city or town where a ship can be anchored and passengers or cargo can go ashore

vessel (VEH sul) — a boat or ship

INDEX

FURTHER READING

Find out more about cruise ships with these helpful books:

• Butterfield, Moira. *Look Inside Cross Sections Ships.* Dorling Kindersley, 1994
• Graham, Ian. *Boats, Ships, Submarines and Other Floating Machines.* Kingfisher, 1993
• Humble, Richard. *Submarines and Ships.* Viking, 1997